50 Flashcards $7.95

Flashcards

FLORIDA
High School
MATHEMATICS

Preparing Students for
FCAT and Sunshine
State Standards

Printed in USA. Minimal packaging for a healthy environment.

©2005 Hollandays Publishing Corporation

HOLLANDAYS
Publishing Corporation

D11136882

Find the surface area of the following rectangular solids.

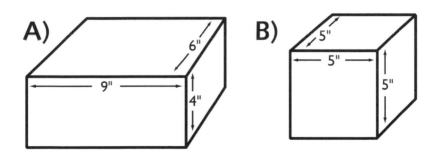

A)

9" 6" 4"

B)

5" 5" 5"

1

A) $36 + 36 + 24 + 24 + 54 + 54 =$
228 square inches

B) $25 \times 6 = 150$ square inches

Identify the two-dimensional figures that make up each object. Then, describe how to find the surface area of the following objects. Use the concepts of circumference and area.

1) Prism

2) Cylinder

2

1) A **prism** has a two-dimensional figure (i.e. square, rectangle, triangle or any regular polygon) as a base. The perimeter of the base with height forms a rectangle for the lateral area. To find the surface area, add the area of the bases and lateral area.
Surface Area = 2 (Base Area) + Lateral Area

2) A **cylinder** has two circular bases wrapped by a rectangle. The circumference of one of the circular bases is the length of the rectangle. The width of the rectangle is the height of the cylinder. To find the surface area of a cylinder, add the areas of the two circular bases to the area of the rectangle.

Complete the table.

Fraction	Decimal	Percent
		45%
	0.2	
4/5		
	0.36	
		70%
7/8		

3

Fraction	Decimal	Percent
$\frac{9}{20}$	0.45	45%
$\frac{1}{5}$	0.2	20%
$\frac{4}{5}$	0.8	80%
$\frac{9}{25}$	0.36	36%
$\frac{7}{10}$	0.7	70%
$\frac{7}{8}$	0.875	87.5%

1) When two triangles are similar, corresponding angles are _____ and corresponding sides are _____.

2) When two triangles are congruent, corresponding angles are _____ and corresponding sides are_____.

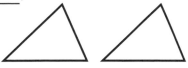

1) equal; in proportion

2) equal; equal in length

Give an algebraic expression for the following:

1) The value of x dimes and y nickels

2) The perimeter of a parallelogram with sides a and b

3) The average of c, d and e

4) The area of a rectangle with length (t) and width (u)

1) $0.10x + 0.05y$

2) $2a + 2b$

3) $(c + d + e) \div 3$

4) $(t)(u)$

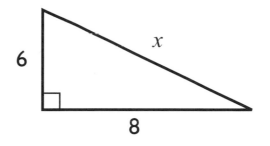

1) Set up the equation to solve for x. Use the Pythagorean Theorem: $a^2 + b^2 = c^2$

2) Solve for x.

6

$$8^2 + 6^2 = x^2$$
$$64 + 36 = x^2$$
$$100 = x^2$$
$$10 = x$$

1) Define and tell how to find the slope of line *l*.

    a) from the graph   **b)** from the equation

2) Define and tell how to find the y-intercept of the line.

    a) from the graph   **b)** from the equation

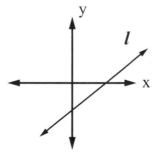

1) a) Pick two points on the line. Count the vertical distance (rise) and the horizontal distance (run) between the two points. Slope $=$ rise $\div$ run

   b) Convert the equation to slope-intercept form. Equation: $y = mx + b$; m is the slope

2) a) The point where the line crosses the y-axis is the y-intercept.

   b) Convert the equation to slope-intercept form. Equation: $y = mx + b$; b is the y-intercept

Choose the correct expression.
Prices for movie tickets are $5 for adults and $2 for children. Which expression represents the total cost for a group of a adults and c children to attend the theater?

a) $7 + a + c$

c) $5a + 2c$

b) $5a + c$

d) $7(a + c)$

How much would it cost for a family of one adult and two children to attend the theater?

c) $5a + 2c$

$5a + 2c = $ Total cost
$5(1) + 2(2) = $ Total cost
Total cost $= \$9$

It would cost $9 for one adult and two children to attend the theater.

1) What methods can you use to solve a system of equations?

2) Solve the system of linear equations by any method.

$$x + y = 5$$
$$x - y = 3$$

1) • Graphing
   • Substitution to eliminate a variable
   • Linear combination
     (add/subtract/multiply/divide)
   • Matrices

2) (4,1)

Similar Triangles
△ ABC ~ △ XYZ

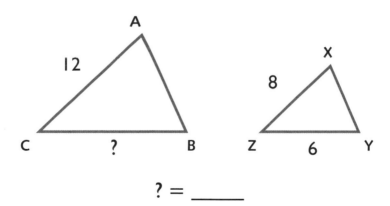

? = _____

10

Similar triangles have sides that are in proportion to each other.

Cross multiply to solve.

$$\frac{8}{12} = \frac{6}{?}$$

? = 9

Solve the system of equations using a matrix:

$$x + y = 10$$
$$x - y = 6$$

11

$$\begin{pmatrix} 1 & 1 & \vdots & 10 \\ 1 & -1 & \vdots & 6 \end{pmatrix} \overset{1.}{=} \begin{pmatrix} 2 & 0 & 16 \\ 1 & -1 & 6 \end{pmatrix} \overset{2.}{=} \begin{pmatrix} 1 & 0 & 8 \\ 1 & -1 & 6 \end{pmatrix}$$

$$\overset{3.}{\begin{pmatrix} 1 & 0 & 8 \\ 0 & -1 & -2 \end{pmatrix}} \overset{4.}{=} \begin{pmatrix} 1 & 0 & \vdots & 8 \\ 0 & 1 & \vdots & 2 \end{pmatrix} \qquad \begin{aligned} x &= 8 \\ y &= 2 \end{aligned}$$

1. Add bottom row to top.
2. Divide top row by 2.
3. Multiply top row by -1. Add top row to bottom.
4. Multiply bottom row by -1

Consider these numbers:

1) 0.00456   **2)** 9380000

a) Explain how to convert each number to scientific notation.

b) Express each number in scientific notation.

1) a) Move the decimal point three places to the right (4.56). Since the original number was less than one and the decimal point was moved three places, the exponent would be -3.

b) Answer: 4.56×10^{-3}

2) a) Move the decimal point six places to the left. Since the original number was greater than 10 and the decimal point was moved six places, the exponent would be 6.

b) Answer: 9.38×10^{6}

1) Explain the process used to convert a linear equation to slope-intercept form.

2) Tell the relationship of the slopes of two lines if they are:

   a) parallel

   b) perpendicular

1) Solve the equation for y and arrange the equation in slope-intercept form, $y = mx + b$

2) a) Slopes are equal.

b) Slopes are negative reciprocals of each other.

Example: If the slope of one line is $\frac{2}{3}$, the slope of a line perpendicular to it is $-\frac{3}{2}$.

1) Explain how to compare these real numbers.

$$4.65 \times 10^{-2}, \ .01\%, \ \frac{9}{100}, \ 0.06\overline{3}, \ 0.053615...$$

2) Arrange the numbers in descending order.

1) Convert to decimal form, then compare.

2) $\frac{9}{100}$, $0.06\overline{3}$, $0.053615...$, 4.65×10^{-2} , $.01\%$

$$a = 2, \quad b = 1, \quad c = 0$$

Evaluate:

A) $(3b^c)^a$

B) $a^b\sqrt{(b)}$

C) $(2^a - 3^b)^c$

Answers:
- A) 9
- B) 2
- C) 1

1) What is the formula to find the
   area of a triangle?

2) What is the area of this triangle?

3) What is the perimeter
   of this triangle?

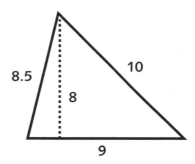

1) The formula for the area of a triangle is base × height ÷ 2
(hint: height = altitude)

2) The area of the triangle is 36 square units.

3) 27.5 units

Define:

1) mean   2) median

3) mode   4) range

5) The first three terms are referred
   to as _____.

6) Which measure of central
   tendency is affected most by
   extremes in data?

1) The **mean** is the arithmetic average of a set of numbers.

2) After arranging the data values in order, the **median** is the middle value.

3) The **mode** is the value or values that occur most often in a data set.

4) The **range** is the distance between the highest and lowest values in a data set.

5) measures of central tendency

6) mean

Explain what happens to a figure when
the following transformations take place:

1) Rotation

2) Reflection

3) Translation

4) Dilation

18

1) Each point of the figure is moved through the same angle. (turn) Example: 90° rotation: $(x, y) \rightarrow (-y, x)$

2) Each point of the figure is moved through a mirror image. (flip) Example: over x-axis: $(x, y) \rightarrow (x, -y)$

3) Every point of the image is moved the same distance in the same direction. (slide) Example: $(x, y) \rightarrow (x + a, y + b)$

4) The image keeps the same shape but changes size. (enlarge/reduce) Example: $(x, y) \rightarrow (kx, ky)$

Simplify.

1) $\sqrt{25}$

2) $\sqrt{200}$

3) $\sqrt{72x^2y^3z^5}$

1) 5

2) $10\sqrt{2}$

3) $6xyz^2\sqrt{2yz}$

Simplify.

Which law of exponents is used in each?

1) $2^3 \cdot 2^{10} = 2^{13}$

2) $\dfrac{2^{10}}{2^3} = 2^7$

3) $(2^3)^{10} = 2^{30}$

1) 2^{13}

When multiplying like bases, add exponents.

2) 2^7

When dividing like bases, subtract exponents.

3) 2^{30}

An exponent raised to a power is multiplied by the power.

Match each step in the following solution to the property used.

$$2(3x + 1) + 5x = 24$$

Step 1: $6x + 2 + 5x = 24$ __addition property

Step 2: $2 + 6x + 5x = 24$ __identity property

Step 3: $2 + 11x = 24$ __division property

Step 4: $2 + (-2) + 11x = 24 + (-2)$ __additive inverse

Step 5: $0 + 11x = 22$ __addition property of equality

Step 6: $11x = 22$ __commutative property

Step 7: $x = 2$ __distributive property

$$2(3x + 1) + 5x = 24$$

Step 1: distributive property
$$6x + 2 + 5x = 24$$

Step 2: commutative property
$$2 + 6x + 5x = 24$$

Step 3: addition property
$$2 + 11x = 24$$

Step 4: addition property of equality
$$2 + (-2) + 11x = 24 + (-2)$$

Step 5: additive inverse
$$0 + 11x = 22$$

Step 6: identity property
$$11x = 22$$

Step 7: division property
$$x = 2$$

Simplify.

1) $8x - 3y + 6 \cdot x \div 3 \cdot 4$

2) $\dfrac{(3x^2)}{x} - y^2 - 3x$

1) $16x - 3y$

2) $-y^2$

Given the following sequences, find the common difference or the common ratio and predict the 10th term.

a) 1, 4, 7, 10...

b) 2, 6, 18, 54...

a) common difference = 3;

  10th term = 28

  (1, 4, 7, 10, 13, 16, 19, 22, 25, 28)

b) common ratio = 3;

  10th term = 39,366

  (2, 6, 18, 54, 162, 486, 1458, 4374, 13122, 39366)

Rudy has x CDs. Audra has four more than three times Rudy's.

1) Write the equation in functional notation describing the situation.

2) Make a table of values for $x = 1, 3, 5$.

3) Graph the equation.

1) $f(x) = 3x + 4$

2)

x	y
1	7
3	13
5	19

3)

The graph shows the sales trend for the first three weeks of a local band's album release.

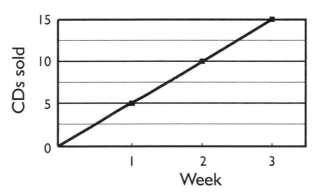

How are the sales changing? At what rate?

The sales are increasing at a rate of about 5 CDs a week.

Beth is going to paint the floor of her L-shaped swimming pool.

How many square feet of paint will Beth apply?

What is the volume of her pool if it averages 5 ft deep?

Beth will need 208 ft^2 of paint.

The volume of the pool is 1040 ft^3.

Point **A**, Point **B**, and Point **C** are collinear.

A = (3, 3)
B = (0, 1)
C = (-3, -1)

What is the slope of the line?

Select two points (for example, A and C)

$$m = \frac{y}{x}$$

$$m = \frac{(y_2 - y_1)}{(x_2 - x_1)}$$

$$m = \frac{(-1 - 3)}{(-3 - 3)}$$

$$m = \frac{-4}{-6} \qquad m = \frac{4}{6} \text{ or } \frac{2}{3} \qquad \text{The slope is } \frac{2}{3}$$

1) Define and describe the **line of best fit** in a scatterplot.

2) How do you find the slope of the line of best fit in a scatterplot?

3) What kind of correlation is illustrated in each data set below?

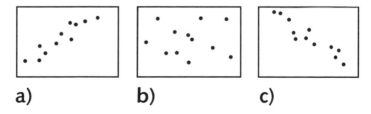

a)   b)   c)

1) A **line of best fit** is a trend line that most closely represents the data on a scatterplot.

2) Pick two points on the line of best fit. Determine the slope by finding the value of the rise ÷ run.

3)   **a)** Positive correlation
      b) No correlation
      c) Negative correlation

Multiply the following:

a) $3(x + 2)$

b) $(x + 3)(x + 2)$

c) $(2x - 1)(3x - 5)$

d) $(x + 3)(x - 3)$

a) $3x + 6$

b) $x^2 + 5x + 6$

c) $6x^2 - 13x + 5$

d) $x^2 - 9$

Define **absolute value.**

Simplify:

a) $|3| =$ _____

b) $|-3| =$ _____

c) $3\,|-3| =$ _____

d) $\dfrac{|-3|}{3} =$ _____

An absolute value represents a value's distance from zero.
This value is always positive.

a) 3   b) 3   c) 9   d) 1

Solve:

a) $3x - 2x + 5 = 15 - 3$

b) $x + 9x - 6x = 20 - 4$

a) $3x - 2x + 5 = 15 - 3$

$x + 5 = 12$

$x + 5 - 5 = 12 - 5$

$x = 7$

b) $x + 9x - 6x = 20 - 4$

$10x - 6x = 16$

$4x = 16$

$x = 4$

Mr. Houston drove 60 miles in 1¼ hours. Answer the following questions about Mr. Houston's trip.

a) What formula can you use to find Mr. Houston's speed?

b) Mr. Houston's average speed was _____ miles per hour.

c) At the same speed, how far will Mr. Houston travel in three hours?

a) Distance = rate × time

b) Distance = rate × time

60 = rate × 1.25

60 ÷ 1.25 = rate

rate = 48 miles per hour

c) 48 × 3 = 144 miles

Find two positive numbers with a product of 120 and a difference of 2.

33

$x\,y = 120$
$x - y = 2$

$x = y + 2$
$(y + 2)\,(y) = 120$
$y^2 + 2y - 120 = 0$
$(y + 12)\,(y - 10) = 0$
$y = -12,\ 10\ ;\ -12$ is not positive
$y = 10;$ therefore, $x = 12$

The numbers are 12 and 10

Find the volume of the following rectangular solids:

a)

b)

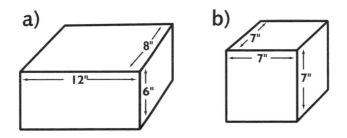

a) 576 cubic inches

b) 343 cubic inches

What is the difference between a **combination** and a **permutation**?

a) Greg tosses a two-sided coin twice. How many **combinations** of heads and tails can he get as a result?

b) How many **permutations** can he get?

Combination: order of terms does not matter
Permutation: order of terms matters

a) Greg can have 3 different combinations: H,H T,T
   and H,T *or* T,H (T,H and H,T are considered the
   same combination because order does not matter)

b) Greg can get 4 different permutations: H,H T,T
   H,T *and* T,H (H,T and T,H are considered two
   different permutations because order does matter)

Match

1) Area of a rectangle
2) Volume of a cube
3) Surface area of a cube
4) Length of the side of a rectangle
5) Volume of a pyramid
6) Surface area of a prism
7) Circumference of a circle
8) Diameter of a circle
9) Volume of a sphere
10) Perimeter of a trapezoid

A) Square feet (ft^2)

B) Cubic feet (ft^3)

C) Feet (ft)

1) A
2) B
3) A
4) C
5) B
6) A
7) C
8) C
9) B
10) C

Linear measure is measured in feet; area is measured in square feet; volume is measured in cubic feet.

The teacher has a sack filled with candy bars. He has 10 Chocos, 5 Mint Cups, 8 Twinbars, and 7 Peanut Clusters. What is the probability that a student will pick each candy bar below?

1) Chocos
2) Mint Cups
3) Twinbars
4) Peanut Clusters

1) 10/30 = 1/3

2) 5/30 = 1/6

3) 8/30 = 4/15

4) 7/30

Simplify:

1) -4×3

2) $-8 \div 2$

3) 3×-2

4) $25 \div 5$

5) -6×-3

6) When multiplying and/or dividing positive and negative numbers, if both numbers have the same sign, the answer is _____; however, if the two numbers have different signs, the answer is _____.

1) -12

2) -4

3) -6

4) 5

5) 18

6) positive; negative

Convert the decimals to fractions reduced to lowest terms.

1) .8

2) .31

3) .179

4) .35

1) $\dfrac{4}{5}$

2) $\dfrac{31}{100}$

3) $\dfrac{179}{1000}$

4) $\dfrac{7}{20}$

Given: Circle **M**

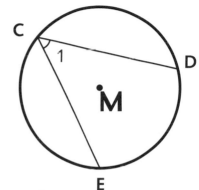

1) ∠1 is called a(n) _____ angle.

2) What is the intercepted arc?

3) How do you find the $m\angle 1$?

1) inscribed

2) The intercepted arc runs from D to E through the interior of the inscribed angle.

3) The measure of an inscribed angle is one half the measure of its intercepted arc.
$m \angle 1 = \frac{1}{2} m \overset{\frown}{DE}$

Explain how to establish that quadrilateral ABCD in the coordinate plane is a parallelogram.

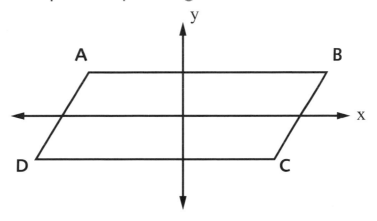

A parallelogram is defined as a quadrilateral with opposite sides parallel.

To establish that opposite sides are parallel, use the slope formula to prove that $\overline{AB} \parallel \overline{CD}$ and $\overline{AD} \parallel \overline{BC}$. If the slopes of two sides are equal, then those sides are parallel.

Inverse Variation

1) Describe inverse variation.

2) If $y = 6$ when $x = 2$,
find y when $x = 4$

1) If the product of two quantities remains the same (constant), they have an inverse variation relationship. To get the same result, one quantity increases while the other quantity decreases. *You can say that "y varies inversely with x" or "y is inversely proportional to x."*

Equation: $y = \dfrac{k}{x}$ or $k = yx$, where k is constant.

Example: $xy = 4$ or $y = \dfrac{4}{x}$; the graph is not linear.

2) $6 \times 2 = k$

$12 = k$

$4y = 12$

$y = 3$

1) Describe **direct variation**.

2) If $y = 9$ when $x = 2$,
find x when $y = 6$

43

1) If two variables have the same rate or ratio regardless of their values, they have a direct variation relationship.

You can say that "y varies directly with x" *or* "y varies directly as x."

Equation: $y = kx$ or $\dfrac{y}{x} = k$, where k is constant.

Example: $y = 8x$; the equation is a line.

2) $9 = 2k$

$\dfrac{9}{2} = k$

$6 = \dfrac{9}{2}x$

$\dfrac{12}{9} = x$

$1\frac{1}{3} = x$

Give the following formulas and facts about the circle:

1) Define the **diameter**.

2) Define the **radius**.

3) Define the **circumference**.

4) If the radius = 5 cm, C = _____.

1) **Diameter** is the length of a line segment that passes through the center of a circle and connects two points on the circumference.

2) **Radius** is the distance from the center of a circle to any point on the circumference (the perimeter).

3) **Circumference** is the distance around a circle.

4) $C \approx 10 \, (3.14) \approx 31.4 \text{ cm}$
   $C = 10 \, \pi$

1) Explain how to find the average of four numbers.

2) Find the mean and median for the following:

   a) 15, 19, 25, 21, and 13

   b) 7.8, 9.2, 6.5, and 8.1

45

1) Add the numbers and divide the sum by four.

2) a) mean = 18.6   median = 19

Order the numbers (13 15, 19, 21, 25) to determine the answer.

b) mean = $\dfrac{31.6}{4}$ = 7.9

median = $\dfrac{15.9}{2}$ = 7.95

Order the numbers (6.5, 7.8, 8.1, 9.2) to determine the answer.

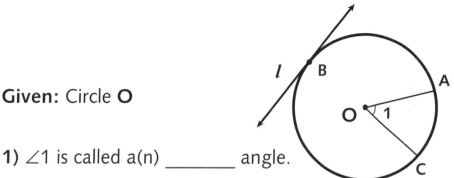

Given: Circle **O**

1) ∠1 is called a(n) _____ angle.

2) Describe the major arc of ∠1.

3) Describe the minor arc of ∠1.

4) How do you find the *m*∠1?

5) Line *l* is called _____?

1) central

2) The major arc is from A to C around the outside of the central angle. Major arc: $\overset{\frown}{ABC}$

3) The minor arc is from A to C through the interior of the central angle. Minor arc: $\overset{\frown}{AC}$

4) The measure of a central angle is the same as the measure of its intercepted arc.
m $\angle 1$ = degree measure of $\overset{\frown}{AC}$

5) tangent

Given the following square pyramid:
a) Find the volume.
b) Find the surface area.

$d = 10$ cm

$b = 8$ cm

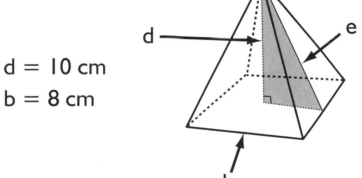

a) $v = \dfrac{8^2(10)}{3}$

$\quad \approx 213.3 \text{ cm}^3$

b) $e = \sqrt{10^2 + 4^2} \approx 10.8$

$\quad SA = 8^2 + 4\,\dfrac{(10.8\,(8))}{2} = 64 + 172.8$

$\quad\quad = 236.8 \text{ cm}^2$

On the graph of a linear inequality, how do you decide:

a) whether the line is solid or dashed

b) where to shade the graph

c) Study the graph, then complete this inequality:
$y \_\_\_ x + 1$

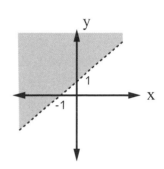

a) If the linear inequality uses a $\geq$ or $\leq$, the graph is a solid line.
If the linear inequality uses a $<$ or $>$, the graph is a dashed line.

b) Pick a point on either side of the graphed line of the inequality.
Substitute the x and y coordinates of that point into the inequality.
- If these substituted values yield a true statement, shade the
graph on the side of the graph where the point is located.
- If the statement is false, shade the side of the graph opposite
the point.

c) $y > x + 1$

Describe the graph:

1) $f(x) = x^2$

2) $f(x) = 3x^2$

3) $f(x) = -x^2$

4) $f(x) = (x - 1)^2$

5) $f(x) = (x - 1)^2 + 2$

1) parabola, opens up, vertex at (0,0)

2) parabola, similar to x^2 but wider, vertex (0,0)

3) parabola, opens down, vertex (0,0)

4) parabola, opens up, vertex (1,0) shifts right

5) parabola, opens up, vertex (1,2) shifts right and up

Use the formula $I = PRT$.

To buy his car, Jason borrowed $3500 from a bank at 12% interest. He decided to borrow the money for two years.

1) How much interest will he pay?

2) What is the total cost of the car?

3) What is his monthly payment?

1) $840

2) $4340

3) $180.83

Matching:

1) a plane intersects a cone, parallel to the base

2) a plane intersects a cone, oblique to the base

3) a plane intersects two right cones stacked vertex to vertex, perpendicular to the bases

4) a plane intersects one cone perpendicular to its base

5) two planes intersect

A) hyperbola

B) parabola

C) circle

D) line

E) ellipse

1) C
2) E
3) A
4) B
5) D